THE BAT FROM HELL

TAKE THAT BOOKS

Take That Books is an imprint of
Take That Ltd.
P.O.Box 200
Harrogate
HG1 2YR

Written and illustrated by Paul Wood

10 9 8 7 6 5 4 3 2 1

ISBN 1-873668-21-X

Layout and typesetting by
Take That Ltd., P.O.Box 200, Harrogate, HG1 2YR.

Printed and bound in Great Britain.

TAKE THAT BOOKS

"Would you like to guess which one is yours?"

"I find it less painful carrying him on my front"

"He looks a lot like his Father"

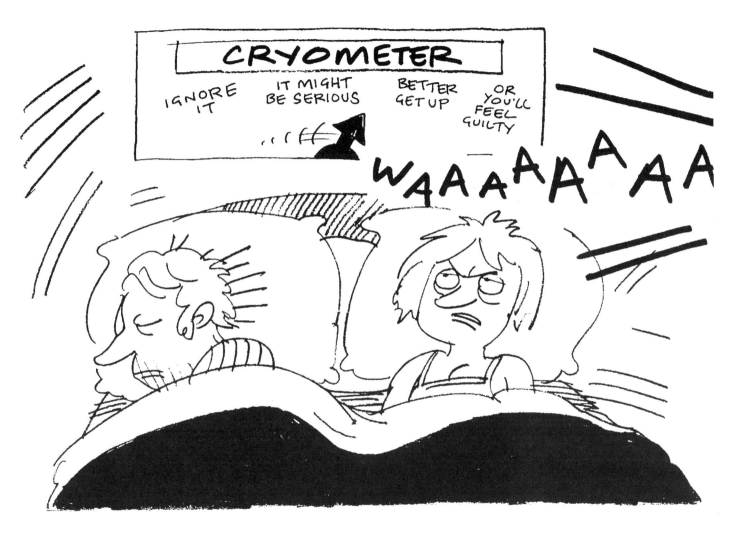

"I can't keep up with his appetite"

"Sorry Puss, Baby's had the last of the milk"

"'I baptise this child
Anthony 'Little-Basket Pain-In-The-Rectum I-Wish-He'd-Shutup' Smith"

"Believe me, it's the best way to put on a nappy"

It's a small world

"Whoops"

Infantry

"He's absolutely mesmerised by the washing machine"

"Maybe it's not violent enough"

"Uh, oh - I think he's going to wet the..."

"Morning"

"I think you've patted Mrs Johnson's dog enough now dear"

Acotalypse Now

"Thanks ever so much for agreeing to babysit for us"

"In the basement? Why would anyone want a nursery in the... Gulp"

Cot Potato

"Can you smell burning?"

"Sleep, sleep"

"He will have his little tantrums"

"Hi, Karen, how's the diet going?"

"Good morning"

"And what do you think you're doing?"

"Did you ever find that used condom?"

"He's very bright for his age"

"Are you sure they're his milk teeth"

"*Have you seen my pep-pills?*"

"Hello, we're back. Was the little love any trouble? ... Hello? ... Hello?"

"Don't you think he's a bit young for adolescence"

Small Talk

"'What big eyes you've got Grandma', said Little Red Riding Hood pulling out her pump-action shotgun"

"Sorry, I can't give you eyes in the back of your head, but I know a specialist who can."

MORE HUMOUR TITLES...

The Ancient Art of Farting *by Dr. C.Huff*
Ever since time began, man (not woman) has farted. Does this ability lie behind many of the so far unexplained mysteries of history? You Bet - because Dr. C.Huff's research shows conclusively there's something rotten about history taught in schools. If you do most of your reading on the throne, then this book is your ideal companion. Sit back and fart yourself silly as you split your sides laughing! *£3.99*

The Hangover Handbook & Boozer's Bible
(In the shape of a beercan)
Ever groaned, burped and cursed the morning after, as Vesuvius erupted in your stomach, a bass drummer thumped on your brain and a canary fouled its nest in your throat? Then you need these 100+ hangover remedies. There's an exclusive Hangover Ratings Chart, a Boozer's Calendar, a Hangover Clinic, and you can meet the Great Drunks of History, try the Boozer's Reading Chart, etc., etc. *£3.99*

Down the Pan: Amuse Yourself in the Toilet
Do you have fun in the toilet? Or, do you merely go about your business and then depart? Instead of staring at the floor and contemplating the Universe, you could be having a ball. Here is an hilarious collection of *cartoons, jokes* and *silly stories...* a gruesome description of *great toilet accidents...* Discover the *secret card tricks* which are certain to impress your friends... Europeans may turn straight to the *Franglais conversation* sur la bog... Look at *famous toilets of history...* Learn how to *juggle toilet rolls*! *£3.99*

For Adult Eyes Only
Sexy stereograms that will keep you up all night.! Here is a collection of naughty pictures you'll just stare at... and stare at... and stare at... Hidden in each of the splashes of colour are racy views, suggestive items and daring positions. Honestly, you just won't believe your eyes - and that's even after you've mastered seeing the stereograms!!! Full Colour. Hardback. *£6.99*

Sex Trivia: A Bedside Companion
Does sex turn you on? Then there's a bedside companion that's titillating, erotic, bizarre, sizzling, shocking, stupendous, hilarious, oddball, staggering... and packed with thousands of TRUE FACTS (all you've ever wanted to know) about your favourite pastime. Find out about... ♥ Killer Condoms ♥ Boomerang Erections ♥ Orgasm as a painkiller ♥ Male Chastity Belts ♥ Sex-aholics Anonymous.. and more! *£3.99*

The Drinking Man's Survival Guide
Discover how to celebrate the joys of drinking... stock up on excuses to get you out of trouble, drink for free... learn to sip and save by making your own beer and wine... make recipes to eat your favourite booze... and meet the world's most amazing drinkers. *£3.99*

A Load of Bollards (for motorists everywhere)
Road cones are about to achieve their galactic mission - to take control of all major road networks. Breeding like rabbits. Moving only at night. Causing chaos as they appear from nowhere. Will the motorists nightmare never end?... *£3.99*

MORE GOOD BOOKS...

The National Lottery Book: Winning Strategies

An indispensable guide to the hottest lottery systems in the world. All designed to help you find those lucky lottery numbers that could make you rich. ● Learn how to Play Like the Pros... ● Discover ways of Getting an Edge... ●Improve your chances with the 'Wheeling Technique'... ● Find possible ways of Making it Happen for you... ● See how understanding betting Psychology and Equitability can seriously Improve Your Winnings... ● Plus lots more General Tips to help you win more! *£4.99*

Postage is FREE within the U.K.
Please add £1 per title in other EEC countries and £3 elsewhere.

Britain's Dumbest Criminals

Hundreds of true stories, from the lad who ran off without paying for an ice-cream and was caught choking on the flake, to the bank robber who left his helmet containing his name and address at a petrol station on the way home. Then there's the woman who tampered with a £200 winning scratchcard to win £20, and the guy who 'posted' himself inside a crate so he could raid a warehouse but didn't pay enough postage. *£4.99*

Mad, Bad Sex

You know it's naughty, but you also know it's nice. If you are short of some ideas then try these for a laugh! *£3.99*

99 Drinking Games for Real Men

A perfect gift book to liven any party or get-together. Have you tried Beer Bungee, Depth Charge, Beeropoly, Fuzzy Duck or Thumper recently? There's card and coin games, adapted board games, General Knowledge games, endurance tests, skill and coordination games, TV/Video related games and much, much more. *£3.99*

Mad Cats and Englishmen

The true stories of mad moggies and their equally lunatic owners from the files of animal behaviourist Peter Neville. Why was Albert deeply in love with the control knob on the radiator? How did Monty come to throw an alcoholic wobbly and attack the Major's wife? Could a Red Persian pass himself off as a statue in the bird bath? And how much damage did Karma cause to her owner's designer clothes after being excluded from the house one night? *£3.99*